Musty-Crusty Animals

Horseshoe Crabs

Lola M. Schaefer

Heinemann Library
Chicago, Illinois

Customer Service 888-454-2279
Visit our website at www.heinemannlibrary.com

Designed by Sue Emerson/Heinemann Library and Ginkgo Creative, Inc.
Printed and bound in the U.S.A. by Lake Book

06 05 04 03 02
10 9 8 7 6 5 4 3 2 1

Library of Congress Cataloging-in-Publication Data
Schaefer, Lola M., 1950-
    Horseshoe crabs / Lola Schaefer.
        p. cm. — (Musty-crusty animals)
Includes index.
Summary: A basic introduction to horseshoe crabs, discussing their
physical characteristics, habitat, activities, and diet.
    ISBN 1-58810-515-6 (lib. bdg.)   ISBN 1-58810-724-8 (pbk. bdg.)
    1. Limulus polyphemus—Juvenile literature. [1. Horseshoe crabs.] I.Title.
    QL447.7 .S33 2002
    595.4'92—dc21

                              2001003284

Acknowledgments
The author and publishers are grateful to the following for permission to reproduce copyright material:
Title page, pp. 6, 13 E. R. Degginger/Color Pic, Inc.; pp. 4, 7, 8, 9, 18, 19 Grace Davies Photography; pp. 5, 14, 15, 22 Jeff Rotman Photography; pp. 10, 12, 16, 17, 20, 21 Dwight Kuhn; p. 11 David Liebman; glossary (helmet) Amor Montes de Oca

Cover photograph courtesy of Grace Davies Photography

Every effort has been made to contact copyright holders of any material reproduced in this book. Any omissions will be rectified in subsequent printings if notice is given to the publisher.

Special thanks to our advisory panel for their help in the preparation of this book:
Eileen Day, Preschool Teacher
Chicago, IL

Paula Fischer, K–1 Teacher
Indianapolis, IN

Sandra Gilbert,
Library Media Specialist
Houston, TX

Angela Leeper,
Educational Consultant
North Carolina Department
of Public Instruction
Raleigh, NC

Pam McDonald, Reading Teacher
Winter Springs, FL

Melinda Murphy,
Library Media Specialist
Houston, TX

Helen Rosenberg, MLS
Chicago, IL

Anna Marie Varakin,
Reading Instructor
Western Maryland College

Special thanks to Dr. Randy Kochevar of the Monterey Bay Aquarium for his help in the preparation of this book.

Some words are shown in bold, **like this.**
You can find them in the picture glossary on page 23.

Contents

What Are Horseshoe Crabs?

Horseshoe crabs are animals without bones.

They are **invertebrates**.

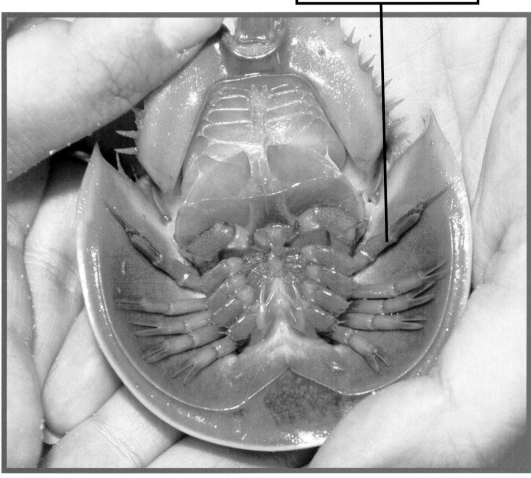

jointed leg

Horseshoe crabs have **jointed legs.**

The legs are for walking and holding food.

Where Do Horseshoe Crabs Live?

Horseshoe crabs live on the ocean floor.

They live in water near land.

Horseshoe crabs come onto land
to build nests and lay eggs.

What Do Horseshoe Crabs Look Like?

tail

Horseshoe crabs look like walking **helmets**.

Their tails are long and pointed.

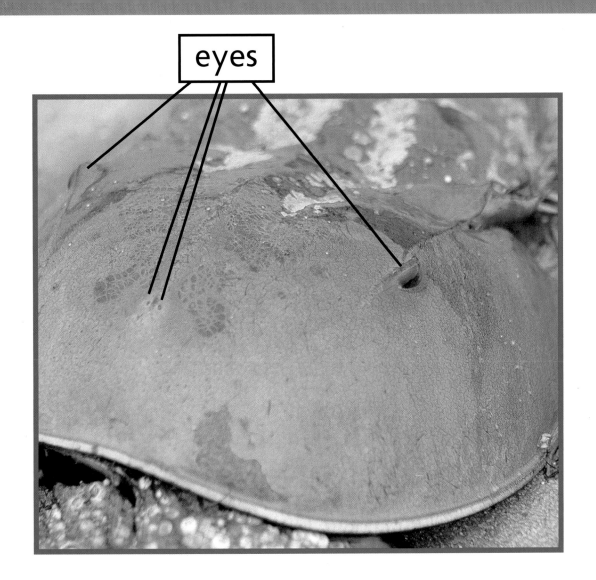

eyes

Most horseshoe crabs are dark green and brown.

Their eyes are on their shells.

Do Horseshoe Crabs Really Have Shells?

People call the hard outsides of horseshoe crabs "shells."

But horseshoe crab shells are really **exoskeletons**.

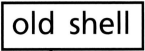

old shell

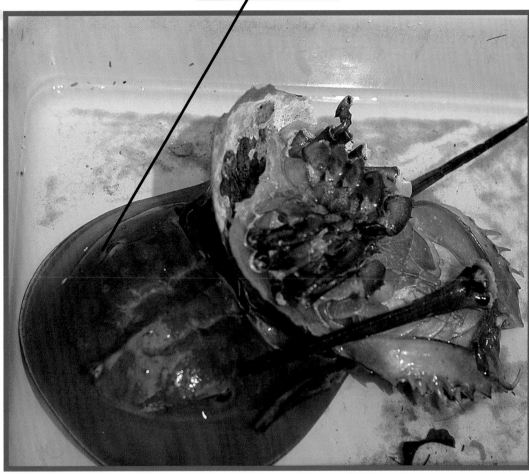

As horseshoe crabs grow, their shells get too small.

The horseshoe crabs leave their old shells and grow new ones.

What Do Horseshoe Crabs Feel Like?

The outsides of horseshoe crabs are bumpy and hard.

spines

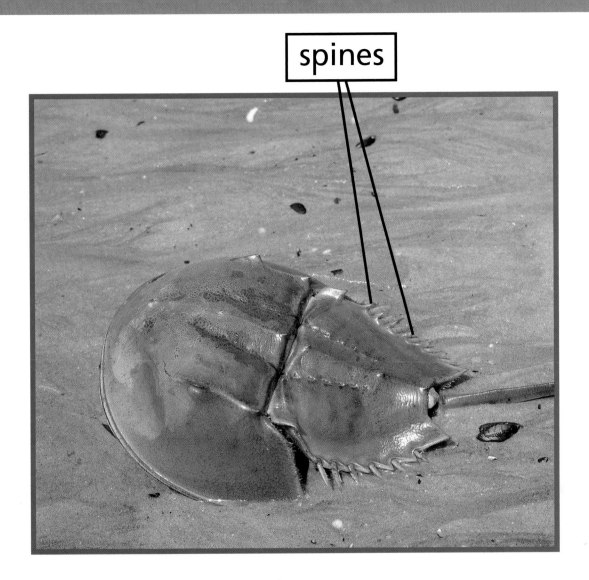

Horseshoe crab **spines** feel sharp.

Their **claws** and tails feel sharp, too.

How Big Are Horseshoe Crabs?

Young horseshoe crabs are a little bigger than a finger.

Adult horseshoe crabs can be very big.

This one is almost as big as this woman.

How Do Horseshoe Crabs Move?

Horseshoe crabs crawl over sand.

They can also swim in the ocean.

Waves can turn horseshoe crabs upside down.

They can use their tails to turn over.

What Do Horseshoe Crabs Eat?

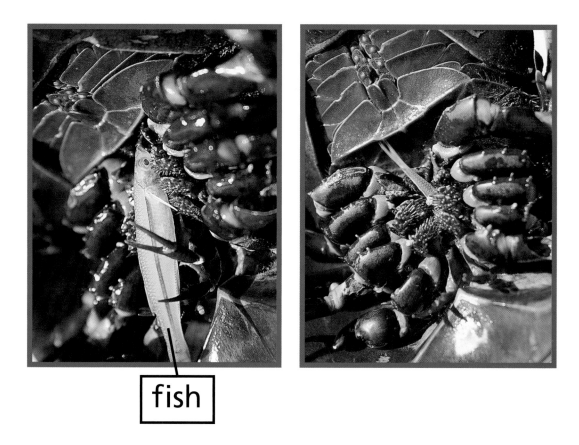

fish

Horseshoe crabs eat live fish.

They eat soft clams and sea worms, too.

Sometimes horseshoe crabs eat dead fish or **seaweed.**

Where Do New Horseshoe Crabs Come From?

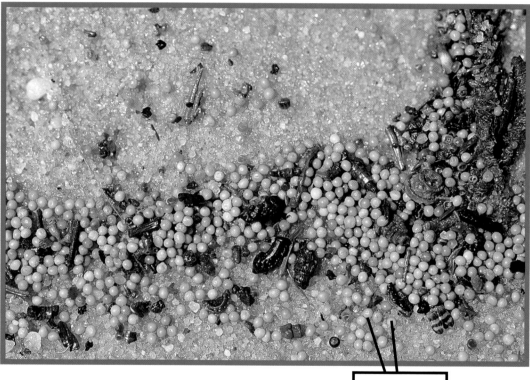

eggs

Female horseshoe crabs dig nests in the sand.

They lay thousands of eggs in each nest.

Little horseshoe crabs come out of the eggs.

They float into the sea.

Quiz

What are these horseshoe crab parts?

Can you find them in the book?

Look for the answers on page 24.

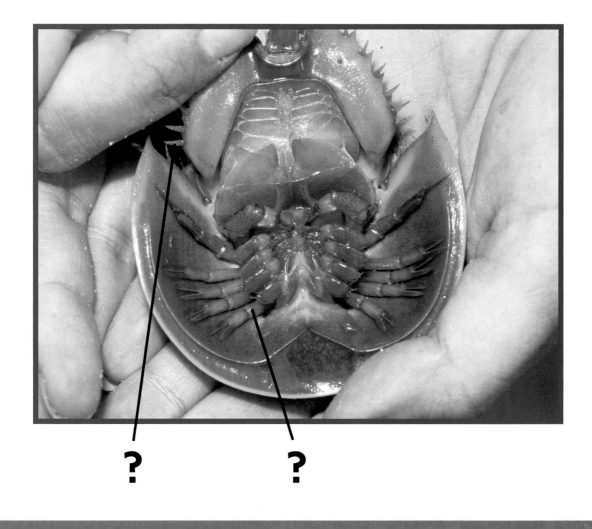

?   ?

Picture Glossary

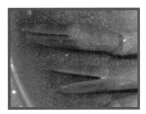 **claws**
page 13

 **jointed legs**
page 5

 **exoskeleton**
(EX-oh-SKELL-uh-tuhn)
page 10

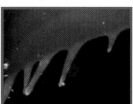 **seaweed**
page 19

 **helmet**
page 8

 **spines**
page 13

 **invertebrate**
(in-VUR-tuh-brate)
page 4

Note to Parents and Teachers

Reading for information is an important part of a child's literacy development. Learning begins with a question about something. Help children think of themselves as investigators and researchers by encouraging their questions about the world around them. Each chapter in this book begins with a question. Read the question together. Look at the pictures. Talk about what you think the answer might be. Then read the text to find out if your predictions were correct. Think of other questions you could ask about the topic, and discuss where you might find the answers. Assist children in using the picture glossary and the index to practice new vocabulary and research skills.

! CAUTION: Remind children that it is not a good idea to handle wild animals. Children should wash their hands with soap and water after they touch any animal.

Index

Answers to quiz on page 22

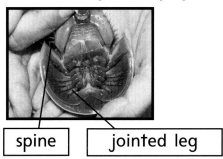

spine | jointed leg